Discovering
the
Caribbean

LEEWARD ISLANDS

ANGUILLA, ST. MARTIN, ST. BARTS, ST. EUSTATIUS, GUADELOUPE, ST. KITTS AND NEVIS, ANTIGUA AND BARBUDA, AND MONTSERRAT

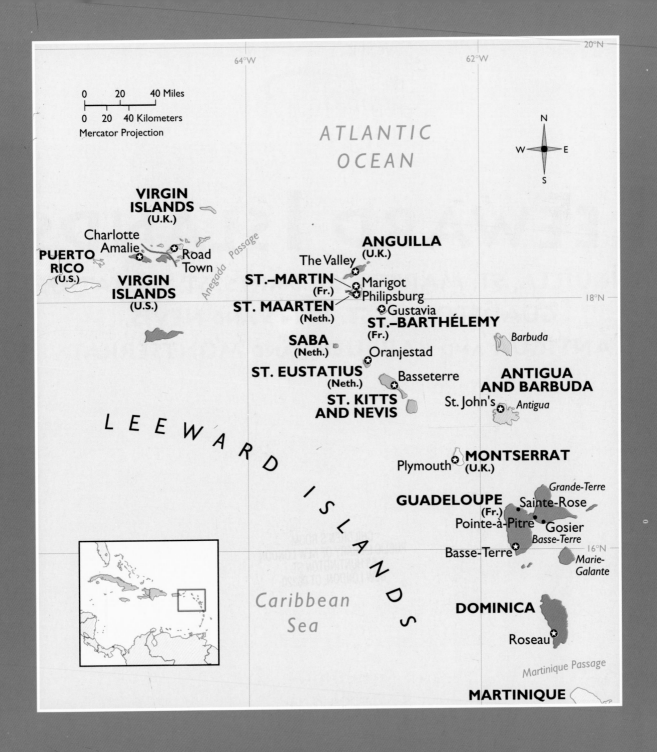

ATLANTIC
OCEAN

N
W • E
S

VIRGIN
ISLANDS
(U.K.)

Charlotte
Amalie
PUERTO
RICO
(U.S.)
VIRGIN
ISLANDS
(U.S.)

Road
Town

Anegada Passage

The Valley

ANGUILLA
(U.K.)

ST.–MARTIN
(Fr.)
ST. MAARTEN
(Neth.)

Marigot
Philipsburg
Gustavia
ST.–BARTHÉLEMY
(Fr.)

Barbuda

SABA
(Neth.)

Oranjestad

ST. EUSTATIUS
(Neth.)

Basseterre

ANTIGUA
AND BARBUDA

ST. KITTS
AND NEVIS

St. John's
Antigua

L E E W A R D   I S L A N D S

Plymouth
MONTSERRAT
(U.K.)

GUADELOUPE
(Fr.)

Grande-Terre
Sainte-Rose

Pointe-à-Pitre
Gosier
Basse-Terre

Basse-Terre

Marie-
Galante

Caribbean
Sea

DOMINICA

Roseau

Martinique Passage

MARTINIQUE

20°N
64°W
62°W
18°N
16°N

0   20   40 Miles
0   20   40 Kilometers
Mercator Projection

Discovering
the
Caribbean

LEEWARD ISLANDS

ANGUILLA, ST. MARTIN, ST. BARTS, ST. EUSTATIUS, GUADELOUPE, ST. KITTS AND NEVIS, ANTIGUA AND BARBUDA, AND MONTSERRAT

Lisa Kozleski

Mason Crest Publishers
Philadelphia

Produced by OTTN Publishing, Stockton, N.J.

Mason Crest Publishers
370 Reed Road
Broomall, PA 19008
www.masoncrest.com

First printing

3 5 7 9 8 6 4 2

Library of Congress Cataloging-in-Publication Data

Kozleski, Lisa.
    The Leeward Islands: Anguilla, St. Martin, St. Barts, St. Eustatius, St. Kitts, Nevis, Antigua,
Barbuda, and Montserrat / Lisa Kozleski.
        p. cm. — (Discovering the Caribbean)
Summary: Presents the geography, history, economy, cities and communities, and people
and culture of the Leeward Islands. Includes recipes, related projects, and a calendar of festivals.
Includes bibliographical references and index.
ISBN 1-59084-307-X
1. Leeward Islands (West Indies)—Juvenile literature. [1. Leeward Islands (West Indies)]
I. Title. II. Series.
F2006 .K69 2003
972.97—dc21

                                                                  2002012355

Discovering
the
Caribbean

Bahamas

Barbados

Cuba

Dominican Republic

Haiti

Caribbean Islands:
Facts & Figures

Jamaica

Leeward Islands

Puerto Rico

Trinidad & Tobago

Windward Islands

Table of Contents

Discovering the Caribbean

James D. Henderson

THE CARIBBEAN REGION is a lovely, ethnically diverse part of tropical America. It is at once a sea, rivaling the Mediterranean in size; and it is islands, dozens of them, stretching along the sea's northern and eastern edges. Waters of the Caribbean Sea bathe the eastern shores of Central America's seven nations, as well as those of the South American countries Colombia, Venezuela, and Guyana. The Caribbean islands rise, like a string of pearls, from its warm azure waters. Their sandy beaches, swaying palm trees, and balmy weather give them the aspect of tropical paradises, intoxicating places where time seems to stop.

But it is the people of the Caribbean region who make it a unique place. In their ethnic diversity they reflect their homeland's character as a crossroads of the world for more than five centuries. Africa's imprint is most visible in peoples of the Caribbean, but so too is that of Europe. South and East Asian strains enrich the Caribbean ethnic mosaic as well. Some islanders reveal traces of the region's first inhabitants, the Carib and Taino Indians, who flourished there when Columbus appeared among them in 1492.

Though its sparkling waters and inviting beaches beckon tourists from around the globe, the Caribbean islands provide a significant portion of the world's sugar, bananas, coffee, cacao, and natural fibers. They are strategically important also, for they guard the Panama Canal's eastern approaches.

The Caribbean possesses a cultural diversity rivaling the ethnic kaleidoscope that is its human population. Though its dominant culture is Latin American, defined by languages and customs bequeathed it by Spain and France, significant parts of the Caribbean bear the cultural imprint of

A newly married couple walks along a peaceful beach on Sint Maarten.

Northwestern Europe: Denmark, the Netherlands, and most significantly, Britain.

So welcome to the Caribbean! These lavishly illustrated books survey the human and physical geography of the Caribbean, along with its economic and historical development. Geared to the needs of students and teachers, each of the eleven volumes in the series contains a glossary of terms, a chronology, and ideas for class reports. And each volume contains a recipe section featuring tasty, easy-to-prepare dishes popular in the countries dealt with. Each volume is indexed, and contains a bibliography featuring web sources for further information.

Whether old or young, readers of the eleven-volume series DISCOVERING THE CARIBBEAN will come away with a new appreciation of this tropical sea, its jewel-like islands, and its fascinating and friendly people!

(Opposite) Boats are docked in the peaceful waters of Bay St. Jean, St. Barts. (Right) Volcanic islands rise above a warm beach in the Leeward group. The islands that make up the Leeward group were created by volcanic activity millions of years ago.

1 The Land

THERE IS A LITTLE bit of paradise to be found on the Leeward Islands, which include Anguilla, Saba, Sint Eustatius, St. Kitts and Nevis, Antigua and Barbuda, Montserrat, St. Martin (which is divided into French St. Martin and Dutch Sint Maarten), St. Barthélemy (St. Barts), and Guadeloupe, which includes seven inhabited islands.

The *archipelago* that is the Leeward Islands is located in the northeastern Caribbean. The word *leeward* is a nautical term that means "sheltered from the wind," and the islands of the Leeward group received this name because of their location in relation to the *trade winds* that blow across the Caribbean. The Leewards make up the northern half of the Lesser Antilles. They are situated in two arcs, running southeast to northwest. The inner ring of islands is composed of volcanoes that are about 15 million years old—a young age by the standards of geological time—and includes the islands from Montserrat to Saba. The outer ring includes a much older string of volcanic islands—about 100 million years old—and includes the islands from Guadeloupe to Anguilla.

While each island has its own history, geology, plant and animal life, and type of government, they all share the warm trade winds of the Caribbean,

A view of Grand Ford from atop Mornede Grand Ford, the highest point on St. Barts.

the constant sunshine, the beautiful *vistas*, and easy access to countless outdoor activities.

The Inviting Caribbean Climate

The climate of the Leeward Islands is, in many ways, ideal. The sun shines almost year-round, and the Caribbean currents keep the water warm. Despite the heat of the sun, the beaches and shorelines are cooled by gentle winds. On the islands, the temperatures of the hot and cold seasons differ by only about five degrees.

Anguilla has a semi-arid climate that is warm year-round. It usually receives about 35 inches (89 centimeters) of rain a year, most falling between October and December. The island's average monthly temperature is 80° Fahrenheit (27° Celsius).

St. Martin, which is the smallest landmass in the world shared by two nations—in this case France and the Netherlands—is tropical year-round, with an average winter temperature of 80°F. It is warmer and more humid in the summer, and the island receives about 45 inches (114 cm) of rain each year. The temperature on St. Barts ranges from 72°F to 86°F (22°C to 30°C), and the island receives about 300 days of sunshine a year. Temperatures on Saba and Sint Eustatius range from a high of about 82°F (28°C) in the summer to a low of about 60°F (16°C) in the winter, and the islands receive about 42 inches (107 cm) of rain each year.

The average temperature on St. Kitts and Nevis is 79°F (27°C), and the islands receive an average of 55 inches (140 cm) of rain during the year. The temperature on Antigua and Barbuda ranges from 76°F (24°C) in January to

83°F (29°C) in August, and the islands receive about 40 inches (102 cm) of rain each year. Guadeloupe's wet season stretches into November; annual rainfall is about 71 inches (180 cm).

A Diverse Terrain

The land of the Leeward Islands is as diverse as the wildlife and plants found on them. Anguilla, one of the driest islands, is very flat. The highest point on the island is just 213 feet (65 meters) above sea level. There are 12 miles (19 kilometers) of powdery beaches around the island's edge, and 33 beaches and caves and seven islets and *cays* that offer diving, snorkeling, and other outdoor activities. In contrast, the island of St. Martin is rugged, made up mostly of steep volcanic hills and pleasant beaches. The highest point on the island juts nearly 1,200 feet (366 meters) above sea level, offering an impressive view of the neighboring islands.

St. Barts is hilly and rugged as well, but also includes wooded areas with low-growing foliage. The beaches of St. Barts are made of white and gold sand. St. Kitts is a volcanic island with a dormant volcano called Mount Liamuiga rising 3,792 feet (1,157 meters) above sea level. The volcano is home to a tropical rain forest and rare animals and plants. Steep hills wind their way around the small island of Nevis, where the highest point is Nevis Peak, at 3,232 feet (986 meters) above sea level.

With a total area of 688 square miles (1,780 sq km), Guadeloupe is the largest member of the Leeward Islands. It is composed of two medium-sized islands, Basse-Terre and Grand-Terre, as well as a number of smaller islands: Marie-Galante, La Desirade, two tiny islands known collectively as Iles des

Rolling, grassy hills in the interior of Antigua.

Saintes, and Iles de la Petite Terre. Basse-Terre's highest peak, on Mount La Grande Soufriére, measures 4,813 feet (1,467 meters) and is the highest point of the Lesser Antilles chain.

Quick Facts: The Geography of the Leeward Islands

Location: The northern islands of the Lesser Antilles, in the Caribbean

Area:
Anguilla: 39 square miles (102 sq km)
Antigua: 108 square miles (280 sq km)
Barbuda: 62 square miles (161 sq km)
Guadeloupe[1]: 687 square miles (1,780 sq km)
Montserrat: 39 square miles (102 sq km)
Netherlands Antilles[2]: 371 square miles (960 sq km)
Nevis: 36 square miles (93 sq km)
Saint Kitts: 65 square miles (168 sq km)

Climate: tropical, moderated by northeast trade winds. Many islands face hurricanes in the months between July and October.

Terrain: Anguilla has dry, flat land, and St. Barts is hilly and rugged. All other islands have hilly, volcanic interiors.

Elevation extremes:
lowest point: Caribbean Sea—0 feet
highest point: Grande Soufriére, Guadeloupe—4,810 feet (1,467 meters)

Natural hazards: hurricanes and tropical storms, volcanoes

[1] includes Basse-Terre, Grande-Terre, Marie-Galante, La Desirade, the two Iles des Saintes, Saint-Barthélemy, Iles de la Petite Terre, and Saint Martin.
[2] includes Saba, Sint Eustatius, Sint Maarten, Bonaire, and Curaçao.

Source: Adapted from CIA World Factbook 2002.

Guadeloupe, French St. Martin, and St. Barts together form a unified territory of France called a *département*. However, St. Barts and St. Martin will be treated separately from Guadeloupe in this book because they are located about 150 miles (240 km) to the north and because of their size.

Sint Maarten, located on the southern part of the island of St. Martin, is a territory of Holland. It is part of a Dutch administrative group called the

Netherlands Antilles. The Netherlands Antilles also includes Saba and Sint Eustatius, as well as two islands located to the south, Bonaire and Curaçao. These two islands are sometimes included with another group of islands in the Lesser Antilles, the Windward Islands. Saba is only about 5 square miles (13 sq km), while Sint Eustatius is about 8 square miles (21 sq km).

Antigua is the second-largest island of the Leewards. It is promoted to tourists as having 365 beaches—one for every day of the year. The island is made of limestone and coral and has rolling hills. Its highest point is Boggy Peak at 1,330 feet (406 meters).

Of the smaller Leeward Islands, Barbuda is best known for its pink sandy beaches. Saba is a steep, mountainous but tiny volcanic island, where the highest point is Mount Scenery (2,885 feet/880 meters). Sint Eustatius is

Tourists walk along one of Saint Martin's beaches. The island covers 37 square miles (96 square kilometers). The island is the smallest landmass to be shared by two separate governments. France controls St. Martin in the north, which covers 21 square miles (54 sq km), while the Netherlands controls St. Maarten, which covers 16 square miles (42 sq km).

The islands of the Leeward group are popular among scuba divers. Many of the islands have coral reefs, underwater caves, or sunken ships that experienced divers can explore. The warm, clear waters around the islands make the sport popular for first-time divers as well.

also a volcanic island with rolling hills. The highest point is the Quill (1,890 feet/577 meters), which is a perfectly shaped volcano, now extinct. Montserrat's Soufriére Hills also have a history of volcanic eruptions. Chances Peak is the island's highest point at 2,999 feet (914 meters). A small coastal lowland lies on the outskirts of Montserrat's volcanic mountains.

An Abundance of Stunning Natural Features

The Leeward Islands are perhaps best known for their beaches, which vary in color, texture, and *topography* from island to island. But the caves, hills, volcanoes, coral reefs, bays, and barrier reefs also distinguish this chain of islands in the middle of the Caribbean. On Anguilla, Shoal Bay is well known for a 2 mile (3.2 km), chalk-white beach that also provides snorkelers reefs to explore. Avid scuba divers can also take advantage of the reefs, boat wrecks, and underwater caves of St. Martin/Sint Maarten. Shell Beach, in the town of Gustavia on St. Barts, is aptly named, as the land is covered with small shells that are nearly identical in shape and size.

St. Kitts, with its huge volcano, rich rain forests, and stunning beaches, is a good place to hike. One trail takes hikers to a place called Black Rocks, which has features made of lava that cooled in the water after sliding from Mount Liamuiga. The cliffs are steep and the winds can be raw along this part of the shore. Hiking is also popular on Nevis. One often-used trail takes walkers on a four-hour trek to the source of the island's freshwater. The trail goes around ravines, through rain forests, and past a waterfall.

Scuba divers on Antigua can find caves and gullies that are home to parrot fish, lobsters, eels, and nurse sharks. The eastern shore of the island of Barbuda contains steep cliffs with many caves, including some carved with Amerindian *petroglyphs*.

(Opposite) The Arawak, a tribe of Amerindians who lived in the Caribbean region, carved petroglyphs like these on several islands in the Leeward group. The Arawak were destroyed by the arrival of Europeans in the 16th century. (Right) Nelson's Dockyard was once a thriving Royal Navy station at English Harbor, Antigua.

2 The History of the Leeward Islands

LIKE THE GEOGRAPHY of the Leeward Islands, the history of the islands is diverse and distinct. (Although each island's story is interesting enough to warrant its own book, this chapter will provide a general history of the Leeward group as a whole, touching on important moments on each island.)

Humans lived on Anguilla long before Columbus ever sailed past the island. The first known residents of this northernmost of the Leeward Islands were the peaceful Arawak Indians, originally from South America. They knew the island as Malliouhana, and left many remnants of their day-to-day life there. Archaeologists believe they had settled at Rendezvous Bay by the sixth century A.D. Anguilla also has a rich history before the Arawak Indians. Archaeologists have found conch shells broken into drinking cups, axes made from shells, flint blades, and other tools from as far back as 1300 B.C., as well as artifacts dating from the fourth century A.D.

Although Columbus probably sailed very near Anguilla in 1493, there is no record of him sighting the flat island. The first Europeans known to have seen the island came in 1565. The French explorer René Laudonnière was probably the first European to formally recognize the island, which he called Anguille (French for "eel") because of its long and thin shape.

Once Europeans began to settle on the island, disease and enslavement led to the deaths of most of the Arawak Indians there. Because of the limited freshwater supplies on Anguilla, settlement and colonization developed

British paratroopers stop civilians on Anguilla, 1969. During the 1960s, the citizens of Anguilla rebelled against an independent union with St. Kitts and Nevis in favor of remaining a British dependency. That status was recognized formally in 1980, and today Anguilla remains a territory of Great Britain.

slowly. Some of the settlers attempted to grow crops and start plantations, using slaves to work the fields until slavery was *abolished* in 1834 throughout the British colonies. The government of Anguilla changed continually over the years, until finally in 1967, the residents rebelled and fought for independence from St. Kitts. The secession became formal in 1980, and today, Anguilla happily exists as a British territory.

St. Martin/Sint Maarten also traces its history back to the Arawak Indians. They called the island Sualouiga, or "Land of Salt," for the *brackish* water that is so visible throughout the island. There are also freshwater springs on this island, which drew the Arawaks to Paradise Peak and other sites. The Arawaks left artifacts at many places. Eventually, they were overwhelmed by the fierce Carib Indians, who gave the region of the Caribbean its name and were also known for practicing *cannibalism*.

During his second voyage to the New World in the fall of 1493, Columbus first spotted an island he named Santa María de Guadalupe. A week later, on November 11, Columbus saw another large island. The day of the sighting was the Roman Catholic feast day of St. Martin, so Columbus decided to name the island after the saint.

Spain and the Netherlands both took an early interest in St. Martin island, and after much battling, Spain eventually left the island to the Dutch, in 1648. But when the Dutch returned to take control of the island, they found French colonists already there. After a brief skirmish, the two nations reached an agreement and divided the island on March 23, 1648.

The settlers on St. Martin soon introduced slavery to the island, hoping to more efficiently cultivate their sugarcane. This system lasted until the

French abolished slavery in 1848 and the Dutch abolished it in 1863. The end of slavery marked the start of a decline in the island's agricultural economy, however, and the island struggled until 1939, when it became a *duty-free port*. Tourism started to develop on Dutch Sint Maarten in the 1950s, and on French St. Martin in the 1970s.

After Columbus sighted the two main islands of Guadeloupe, Spain made a few half-hearted attempts to settle them, but the Carib Indians easily pushed them back. Then the French moved onto Guadeloupe, as they had on nearby St. Martin. By 1635 France had crushed the Caribs and taken possession of the islands.

During the late 18th century and the early 19th century, France and Great Britain fought over Guadeloupe, and the island changed hands several times. In the 20th century, the people of Guadeloupe have gradually received more of the rights of other French citizens. In 1946 the islands of Guadeloupe, together with St. Martin and St. Barts, became a *département*. An elected prefect replaced the French-appointed governor. Since then, the people of Guadeloupe have enjoyed the same level of independence as people living in a *département* in continental France.

Columbus Continues to Leave His Mark

The island of St. Barts was also sighted by Columbus in 1493 and named for the explorer's brother, Bartholomew. The first European settlers were French and arrived in 1648. Just three years later, however, they sold the island to a Roman Catholic religious order called the *Knights of Malta*. Five years after the sale of St. Barts, Carib Indians raided the island and the

Knights of Malta left. St. Barts was left empty until 1673, when the French tried to settle it again. This time, they were successful, helped largely by French **buccaneers**, or pirates.

Because St. Barts did not have a strong agricultural economy, it did not rely on slavery as the other Leeward Islands did. In 1758 the British briefly took over the island, but the French regained control soon afterward. The French sold the island to Sweden in 1784, and nearly 100 years later, in 1878, they bought the island back from the Swedes.

The islands of St. Kitts and Nevis trace their roots back to the Carib Indians. Columbus spotted both islands during his 1493 voyage, naming the larger of the two San Jorge. He later renamed it St. Christopher, after the patron saint of travelers. St. Christopher remains the island's official name today, though the island is more familiarly known as St. Kitts, a nickname given by the British. Columbus first called the smaller island San Martín, but later renamed it Nuestra Señora de las Nieves—Our Lady of the Snows—after the almost ever-present ring of clouds that circled

Christopher Columbus was the first European to see many of the Leeward Islands; many still have the names he gave them on his second voyage in 1493, among them Guadeloupe, St. Martin, Montserrat, and Antigua.

Mount Nevis and gave it a snowcapped look.

In 1623 adventurers from Great Britain came to these islands hoping to build a settlement. A few years later, a French ship joined the British, and the two groups of Europeans banded together to rout the Carib Indians. Later, they again joined forces to defend their settlement from a Spanish attack. But they started fighting against each other in the mid-1600s.

In 1690 a devastating earthquake hit Nevis, and the resulting tidal waves destroyed the capital city and sank a portion of the island. Fighting resumed in the late 18th century. By 1782 the French had won control of St. Kitts, though the British reclaimed it in 1793.

The agricultural economy of both islands relied greatly on slavery. Nevis became the local slave market for many of the neighboring islands. During the 1700s, tens of thousands of slaves worked in the tobacco and sugarcane fields on Nevis, or on the more than 50 sugar plantations operating on St. Kitts. This system lasted until 1834, when slavery was abolished throughout the British colonies. Agriculture continued to thrive, however.

In 1871 the British government placed St. Kitts in a federation with Anguilla, and Nevis joined this group soon after. This was an unhappy marriage, especially for Anguilla, and it ended when the residents of Anguilla rebelled and fought to separate from St. Kitts in the late 1960s. St. Kitts and Nevis became an independent state in 1983, with a prime minister and House of Assembly. In 1998 a *referendum* vote in Nevis on whether to separate from St. Kitts did not receive the two-thirds majority needed to pass.

The first residents of Antigua were the Siboney Indians, who left hand-crafted shell and stone tools that date back to nearly 1800 B.C. After the

Siboney came the Arawak Indians, who arrived on Antigua in about A.D. 35 and stayed until 1100. They were ousted by the Carib Indians, who named the island Wadadli. In 1493 Columbus spotted the island and named it after Santa María de La Antigua of Seville, a saint in whose namesake church he had prayed before setting off on his voyage to the New World.

Because of the fierce Caribs and the lack of freshwater, Europeans stayed away from the island until 1632, when English settlers landed on Antigua and claimed the island for Britain. The relationship between the island and Britain lasted for nearly 350 years.

During the early years of colonization, plantation owners grew sugarcane, but this became unprofitable after slavery was abolished in 1834. About 100 years later, the tourism industry replaced agriculture on the island, and tourism still thrives today.

In 1967 Antigua (along with its sister island, Barbuda) became the first of the eastern Caribbean countries to attain internal self-government as an overseas state of Great Britain. The island achieved full independence in 1981. Although Antigua was battered by Hurricane Luis in 1995, much of the island has since been rebuilt.

Barbuda remained largely unsettled during much of the European settlement of the Leeward Islands. In 1666 the British established a colony there, but it did not thrive. Today, the island is well known as a destination for the rich and famous seeking privacy in a beautiful setting. Britain's Princess Diana often came to Barbuda to take advantage of its *seclusion*. More than 3,000 refugees fleeing a volcanic eruption on Montserrat in 1995 have since settled on Antigua and Barbuda.

Two of the most important figures in the 20th-century history of the Leeward Islands were Robert Llewellyn Bradshaw of St. Kitts (left) and Vere Cornwall Bird of Antigua. Both men were labor leaders, and both were very involved in the formation of the West Indies Federation, an organization intended to unite the islands of the Caribbean economically and politically. Bradshaw (1916—1978) became the first premier of the Associated State of St. Kitts, Nevis, and Anguilla in February 1967. He was a staunch advocate of independence for St. Kitts and Nevis, although this did not occur until five years after his death. Bird (1909—1999) served as chief minister and premier of Antigua before leading his country to independence in 1981, then served as prime minister until 1994.

Small but Still Stunning

The small islands of Saba, Sint Eustatius, and Montserrat have their own unique histories as well. Saba was visited by a shipwrecked crew of Englishmen in 1632 and settled by Dutch explorers in 1640. In 1665 an English pirate named Henry Morgan captured the island and deported everyone who wasn't English. Control of the island changed hands for years, but eventually, in 1816, the Dutch took over. They still govern the island today.

Sint Eustatius, also known as Statia, was settled by the Dutch West India Company in 1636. The main town in Statia was a free port, meaning any ship that came into the harbor to trade was welcome. At its peak, as many as 100 ships might crowd into the port at once. Control of Statia changed hands 22 times during its early years of settlement. Today, Statia is a quiet island with little tourism, although in the early 1990s, cruise ships started docking there. The island is still governed by the Dutch.

The first residents of Montserrat were the Carib Indians, but they were away raiding another island when Columbus arrived during his 1493 voyage and gave the island its full name, Santa María de Montserrate, after an abbey near Barcelona, Spain. The island was settled in 1632 by Europeans, a majority of whom were Irish. Agriculture was the *dominant* part of the economy during the colonial period; the main crops were sugarcane and limes. After slaves were freed in the early 1800s, agriculture declined, and many on Montserrat left to pursue work on other Caribbean islands.

Much of Montserrat was devastated by a volcanic eruption in July 1995; about 8,000 of the island's 12,000 residents fled to neighboring islands to escape the natural disaster. More eruptions in 1996 and 1997 added to the problems. In recent years some people have returned, and Great Britain has started a $123 million aid program to rebuild homes and restore the economy. However, a large part of the island is expected to remain uninhabitable for another decade.

Two views of the popular Dutch resort Sint Maarten. (Opposite) Tourists look for souvenirs on the streets of Philipsburg. (Right) A couple enjoys the scenery from above the beach at Cupecoy. Tourism is one of the most important segments of the economy for all of the islands in the Leeward group.

3 The Economy of the Leeward Islands

HISTORICALLY, THE LEEWARD ISLANDS have had economies based primarily on agriculture. However, during the 20th century tourism became the most important industry on most of the islands. This will probably remain the case for years to come.

The economies of the islands are relatively small—Guadeloupe's is the largest, with a *gross domestic product (GDP)* of about $4 billion a year—but most residents of the islands are fairly well-off. A look at GDP per capita, a measure of each citizen's average share in their country's economy, shows that the residents of most of the islands are in the upper-middle-income range in relation to the rest of the world. The exception is Montserrat, which has not recovered from devastating volcanic eruptions in the 1990s.

Economic Strengths of the Islands

Because Anguilla has few natural resources, tourism plays an especially powerful role in its economy. A sector of the economy that is becoming more important is offshore banking. There is a small amount of farming on the island, and a major agricultural industry is lobster fishing. However, tourism and related jobs in fields such as construction and transportation, employ most of the labor force of Anguilla. The country's GDP in 2001 was $104 million, and the GDP per capita was $8,600.

Throughout its history, Guadeloupe has relied greatly on bananas and sugarcane as exports. This hurt the economy during the 1980s and 1990s, when the market for these products grew unstable. Hurricane Hugo, which devastated the region in 1995, also took a toll on the crops. Tourism has remained a steady source of income, although during the 1980s many visitors to the country were scared off by bombs set off by terrorist groups that wanted to separate the islands from France. Many businesses on Guadeloupe depend greatly on France for aid. However, according to the most recent figures available (1997), Guadeloupe's GDP was the highest among the Leeward Islands at $3.7 billion, and it had a GDP per capita of $9,000.

Sint Maarten, Sint Eustatius, and Saba are three Leeward Islands included in the Netherlands Antilles. Tourism is a mainstay of the economy of the Netherlands Antilles; also vital are *petroleum* shipping and offshore banking. The islands boast a high per capita income ($11,400) and, compared with other countries in the area, have a well-developed infrastructure. Because of poor soil and water supplies, agriculture does not play a *prominent* role in

Workers press sugarcane to make juice on Saba. Sugar processing remains a mainstay of the economies of many islands in the Leeward group.

the economy. The gross domestic product of the Netherlands Antilles, which also includes Curaçao and Bonaire, was $2.4 billion in 2000. Eighty-six percent of the labor force of 89,000 is employed in the service industry, according to recent studies.

Quick Facts: The Economy of the Leeward Islands

Gross domestic product (GDP*):
  Anguilla: $104 million (2001)
  Antigua and Barbuda: $674 million (2000)
  Guadeloupe¹: $3.7 billion (1997)
  Montserrat: $31 million (1999)
  Netherlands Antilles²: $2.4 billion (2000)
  St. Kitts and Nevis: $339 million (2001)
Natural resources: Few besides beaches attracting tourists. Guadeloupe and Saint Kitts and Nevis have arable land. Anguilla has salt and lobster.
Agriculture: cotton, tropical fruits and vegetables, livestock products, cattle, pigs, goats.
Services: tourism, offshore banking.
Industry: construction, cement, rum, sugarcane, sugar processing, boat building, offshore financial services, textiles, light manufacturing.

Foreign trade:
  Exports: bananas, sugar, rum (Guadeloupe); lobster, fish, livestock, salt (Anguilla); machinery, food, electronics, beverages, tobacco (Saint Kitts and Nevis); petroleum, machinery, transport equipment (Antigua and Barbuda); textiles, electronic appliances (Montserrat).
  Imports: foodstuffs, fuels, vehicles, clothing and other consumer goods (Guadeloupe); machinery, manufactures (Saint Kitts and Nevis); chemicals, oil (Antigua and Barbuda); transportation equipment (Montserrat).
Currency exchange rate:
  U.S. $1 = 1.003 Euros (Guadeloupe, St. Barts, and St. Martin, 2003)
  U.S. $1 = 1.790 Netherlands Antillean guilders (Sint Maarten, Sint Eustatius, and Saba, fixed rate since 1989)
  U.S. $1 = 2.7 East Caribbean dollars (Anguilla, Saint Kitts and Nevis, Antigua and Barbuda, and Montserrat, fixed rate since 1976)

¹ includes Basse-Terre, Grande-Terre, Marie-Galante, La Desirade, the two Iles des Saintes, Saint-Barthelemy, Iles de la Petite Terre, and Saint Martin.
² includes Saba, Sint Eustatius, Sint Maarten, Bonaire, and Curaçao.
*GDP = the total value of all goods and services produced in a year.
Source: Adapted from the CIA World Factbook 2002.

The islands of St. Kitts and Nevis traditionally relied on the sugarcane industry as the mainstay of the economy, but tourism, manufacturing, and offshore banking have played much larger roles in recent years. Today, more than 70 percent of the workforce is employed in service-related jobs, and over 25 percent in manufacturing; less than 3 percent are employed in agriculture. The gross domestic product on the two islands was $339 million in 2001, and the GDP per capita was a healthy $8,700.

A woman embroiders a tapestry with a design of two cats at her workshop in Plymouth, Montserrat.

A man weighs fish in the market at Marigot, French St. Martin.

The Potent Power of Tourism

Tourism continues to be the most important industry on the islands of Antigua and Barbuda, accounting for more than half of the gross domestic product of $674 million (2000). The islands were once a haven for clients interested in offshore banking, but new financial sanctions imposed by the United States and the United Kingdom in 1999 hurt the industry. Limited water supplies and labor shortages have made agriculture difficult on the two islands. The labor force of 30,000 is largely employed in commerce and services—about 82 percent have jobs in these fields. The GDP per capita of Antigua and Barbuda is about $10,000.

The economy on the island of Montserrat was devastated by the volcanic activity of the late 1990s. Two-thirds of the 12,000 residents fled the island during those years, and the gross domestic product dropped to $31 million by 1999. The volcanic eruptions crippled the farm industry by damaging crops and making existing land unsuitable for farming. In 1999 construction was the dominant industry, contributing to about one-fifth of the gross domestic product. The economy was bolstered by more than $100 million in aid from the United Kingdom in the late 1990s, but the future of the island's economy remains uncertain.

(Opposite) Three men play a pickup game of cricket on St. Kitts. The modern traditions of the Leeward Islands have been greatly influenced by European, African, and native cultures. (Right) Colorfully costumed dancers prepare for a festival on Nevis.

4 The Culture and People of the Leeward Islands

THE PEOPLE WHO make the Leeward Islands their home are as diverse as the islands themselves. A small number of people living on each island can trace their roots back to pre-Columbian native groups such as the Arawak and Carib Indians. A larger percentage of the people living on the islands today are the descendants of the European settlers who came in the 16th and 17th centuries. The travelers hailed from all over Europe, and ownership and governance of the land changed hands often as different groups struggled to maintain control of the small islands.

Six of the Caribbean islands—including the three Leeward Islands of Sint Maarten, Sint Eustatius, and Saba—were predominantly influenced by Dutch settlers. The colonizers from the Netherlands came to the Caribbean with a different goal than their counterparts from Britain, France, and other countries: they were looking for good harbors for trade instead of rich soil for farming. Although much of the Dutch influence in these islands has lessened over the years as the residents have become increasingly more diverse, mailboxes are still painted Royal Dutch red, people still carry guilders and florins in their wallets, and Dutch is still spoken in schools and post offices.

The French also left their mark on the Leeward Islands—especially on Guadeloupe, St. Barts, and St. Martin. Residents and tourists on St. Barts and

Students learn Dutch on Sint Eustatius. Overall, literacy is high among the people of the Leeward Islands group: more than 90 percent of islanders over the age of 15 can read and write.

St. Martin shop at chic French stores such as Yves Saint Laurent and Christian Lacroix, while they take meals at outdoor cafés that look as if they might have been uprooted from a street in Paris. Unlike Great Britain, which encouraged a gradual move to independence for its islands, France has embraced its Caribbean islands, making them part of the republic and giving them the status of an overseas *département*.

The history of European settlement in the Caribbean also includes the history of slavery. Most of the Leeward Islands have large populations of people descended from the African slaves who were brought to the islands to work on sugarcane or tobacco plantations. During the 17th and 18th centuries millions of Africans were brought in chains to the New World, many to the islands of the Caribbean. Today,

A string band performs on Scilly Cay, Anguilla.

Carnival revelers in costume dance in the streets of St. John's, Antigua. Antigua's Carnival is a 10-day festival held each year in late July and early August.

blacks make up the largest percentage of the population of most of the Leeward Islands. They have made great contributions to the music, arts, and culture of the islands.

But some islands do not have as much of an African influence. St. Barts, for example, did not have a plantation economy, so it did not require the slave population that other Caribbean

Quick Facts: The People of the Leeward Islands

Population: 768,828 (total, all islands)

Ethnic groups: black or mixed black majority. Minorities include white, East Indian, Lebanese, Syrian, Carib Amerindian, Asian, and Portuguese.

Age structure:
0—14 years: 26.23%
15—64 years: 64.98%
65 years and over: 8.13%

Population growth rate: 3.12%

Birth rate: 16.72 babies born/1,000 population

Death rate: 6.75/1,000 population

Infant mortality rate: 92.29/1,000 live births

Religions: Roman Catholic, Anglican, other Protestant, Jewish, Hindu, indigenous African.

Life expectancy at birth:
total population: 74.7 years
male: 72.13 years
female: 77.39 years

Total fertility rate: 2.06 children born per woman

Languages: French and Creole patois (Guadeloupe, St. Martin, St. Barts), Dutch (Netherlands Antilles), English (Saint Kitts and Nevis, Anguilla, Antigua and Barbuda, Montserrat), local dialects.

Literacy rate: Between 90% (Guadeloupe) and 98% (Netherlands Antilles).

Except where noted, all figures are averages of 2002 statistics for the Leeward Islands. Adapted from the CIA World Factbook 2002.

islands needed. Even today, very few residents of St. Barts trace their ancestry back to Africa.

Plenty of Fun and Relaxation

The Leeward Islands come alive with music, dance, color, lights, and noise during the different celebrations of Carnival. These multi-day festivals are some of the best times to visit the islands. On Anguilla, Carnival starts on

Flags of the Leeward Islands

Anguilla

Antigua and Barbuda

Montserrat

Netherlands Antilles

Guadeloupe

St. Kitts and Nevis

Note: The flag of Guadeloupe is the French flag.

the first Monday in August and runs to the middle of the month. Among the activities of Carnival are parades, pageants, swimsuit competitions, street dancing, arts and crafts shows, and boat racing, which is the island's most popular sport. On Sint Maarten, Carnival is celebrated after Easter and continues until April 30, which is the birthday of Princess Juliana, mother of

Queen Beatrix of the Netherlands. Activities include parades, food, and music, as well as the Grand Carnival parade. On the French side of the island, Carnival starts just before Shrove Tuesday and ends on Ash Wednesday. It includes parades and the election of a Carnival queen. On St. Barts and Guadeloupe, Carnival is celebrated on the day before Ash Wednesday; it includes parades and parties in Gustavia on St. Barts, and in Pointe-à-Pitre on Guadeloupe. On Ash Wednesday, island residents put an *effigy* of the spirit Vaval (King Carnival) on a wooden pile and burn it. In Pointe-à-Pitre, a night parade with torches precedes the burning. Most businesses and shops are closed during the celebration.

On St. Kitts and Nevis, no one holiday or festival dominates the calendar, though horse racing is a regular event at nearly every celebration. Large crowds arrive for these races—the only ones held in the Leeward Islands.

On Antigua and Barbuda, the biggest event of the year is Antigua Sailing Week, held in April. Parties, barbecues, races, balls, and other events help celebrate this annual regatta, one of the largest in the Caribbean. The Carnival celebration in late July commemorates the emancipation of the slaves. Among the activities are pageants, parades, and calypso and steel pan music shows. In late October and early November, the Hot Air Balloon Festival is held on Antigua.

(Opposite) The remains of this colonial-era fort provide a great view of Marigot, a popular spot for tourists and the capital of French St. Martin. (Right) Traffic passes through a street lined with colonial-style homes in St. John's, Antigua. The capital of the island is home to about one-third of Antigua's population.

5 The Cities and Communities

THE CAPITAL TOWN of Anguilla is called the Valley and is found at the center of the island. Government offices, the tourist board, a museum, and restaurants can be found in the Valley. Despite its name, the town sits on the island's highest point, known as Crocus Hill. The fishing and boating headquarters for the island are located down the main road at a village called Sandy Ground.

The capital of French St. Martin is a small town called Marigot. This meandering town, which hugs the waterfront, offers a true mix of French and Caribbean culture. Marigot serves as a ferry landing for trips to and from Anguilla, and it is a port for cruise ships. Visitors to the town enjoy both the traditional open market and chic European shops.

The capital city of Dutch Sint Maarten is Philipsburg, which is built on a thin strip of land between Great Bay and the Great Salt Pond. The Dutch side of the island of St. Martin is more *urban* than the French side, but there is still plenty of open space in which tourists can hike, bike, or sail. Narrow streets connect passages lined with shops in Philipsburg, making the traffic slow going through the capital city at all times of the day.

The capital of tiny Saba is called the Bottom, a quaint town notable for its white walls, red roofs, green shutters, and neat gardens. The town was built in the bottom of a depression—hence the name—that is thought to be the crater of the island's extinct volcano.

The only settlement on Sint Eustatius is called Oranjestad. The settlement is made up of two parts, known as Upper and Lower Town. A 100-foot (31-meter) cliff separates the two sections. When the island was active as a trading port, goods were stored in warehouses in Lower Town, while the traders lived in Upper Town. The two sections are linked by an old walkway that was built in 1803. Today, Lower Town has fallen into disrepair and its buildings are largely *dilapidated*.

Pointe-à-Pitre is the capital of Guadeloupe and is located on the island of Grande-Terre. The city's main attractions are its intriguing museums, its glamorous fashion shops, and its many busy marketplaces. At Marche St. Antoine, the largest of the marketplaces on Grande-Terre, tourists can bargain with vendors for tropical produce, spices, and souvenirs. The village of Basse-Terre, on Basse-Terre island, offers a more relaxed setting and more natural attractions. Visitors attempt to climb the mammoth La Soufriére volcano adjacent to the city.

Small-Town Island Life

On St. Kitts, the capital town is Basseterre, a charming community that is built on a swath of land about 1 mile (1.6 km) wide on the south side of the island. Its streets are lined with stone and wooden West Indian houses, and the entire town is sheltered by the green slopes of Monkey Hill and the South

The harbor at Oranjestad, Sint Eustatius.

A small town sits at the base of Mount Nevis. The white clouds that linger around the top of the mountain inspired Christopher Columbus to name the island Nuestra Señora de las Nieves (Our Lady of the Snows).

Range. Basseterre is home to about half of the island's population, more than 15,000 people. The only important town on neighboring Nevis is also the island's capital, Charlestown. This community is made up of a few streets lined with charming stone buildings memorable for their balconies and *gingerbread woodwork*. About 1,500 of the island's residents live in town, which comes alive whenever the ferry arrives.

Antigua's capital is St. John's, which is built on a region of gently sloping land above a bay. More than one-third of all Antiguans live in or around St. John's, and the town is filled with shops, restaurants, open markets, and fishermen. In nearby Barbuda, the only town is Codrington, named after an English family that leased the whole island as an estate from 1674 to 1870. There are about 1,200 residents on the island, and nearly all of them live in Codrington.

The small capital town of Montserrat is Plymouth, which is built on an open bay on the southwest coast of the island. Before the volcanic activity of the late 1990s, the town boasted a bustling public market and classical British West Indian architecture with multiple levels, shaded balconies, and red tin roofs.

On tiny St. Barts, the capital town is Gustavia. The town was rebuilt after 1850, when a hurricane and fire damaged most of the buildings in Gustavia. The permanent population of Gustavia is now just a few hundred—a small fraction of what it was 200 years ago when the harbor was crammed with ships and the town was filled with merchants and goods.

Each of the Leeward Islands offers a rich assortment of outdoor activities and Caribbean living. And each island has several unusual facts of which it can boast. For instance, according to the book *Adventure Guide to the Leeward Islands*, the monkey population on St. Kitts and Nevis is 2.5 times larger than the islands' human population. Legislators on St. Kitts and Nevis have passed a law decreeing that no building can be taller than a palm tree. The island of Saba is actually the tip of a volcano. And Anguilla calls itself "the Wreck Diving Capital of the Caribbean," as seven wrecked ships surround the island and are upright and accessible to divers of different skill levels.

With their long and rich history, there is much to discover about these gems of the Caribbean known as the Leeward Islands.

A Calendar of Leeward Island Festivals

JANUARY

New Year's Day is celebrated on January 1. The next day on St. Kitts and Nevis is the **Last Lap Festival**.

Other festivals celebrated in the Leeward Islands during the month include **Epiphany** (Three Kings' Day) and **La Fête des Rois**.

During the two-week-long **St. Barts Music Festival**, a variety of music—from opera to jazz to chamber music—is performed.

FEBRUARY

A popular festival is held the day before the Roman Catholic period of **Lent**, which often occurs in February. It is known as **Carnival** or **Mardi Gras**. This joyous celebration is followed by the seriousness of **Ash Wednesday**, which begins the Lenten period. On St. Martin and St. Barts, a day-long respite from fasting called **Mi-Careme** is observed.

St. Kitts and Nevis hosts an annual flower show in February.

MARCH

Christians celebrate Holy Week, culminating with **Easter Sunday**, in March or April each year.

In Sint Maarten/St. Martin on March 23, the anniversary of the **Treaty of Concordia,** in which the French and Dutch agreed to share the island peacefully, is observed.

On St. Barts, the **Arts and Artisans** show of arts and crafts is held in Gustavia.

APRIL

After Easter, another **Carnival** celebration is held until April 30 on Sint Maarten.

During the month St. Barts holds its **Festival Gastronomique**, a presentation of regional wine and cooking, and the St. Barts **Film Fete and Caribbean Cinematheque**, a five-day salute to Caribbean films and filmmakers

MAY

On May 1, people in Anguilla, Sint Maarten/St. Martin, St. Barts, and Guadeloupe commemorate **Labour Day**. Labour Day is observed May 5 on St. Kitts and Nevis, Antigua, and Barbuda.

On May 8, St. Barts commemorates **Armistice Day**.

May 19 is **Whit Monday** on St. Kitts and Nevis and Antigua and Barbuda.

Slavery Abolition Day is observed May 27 on St. Barts and Guadeloupe.

May 30 is **Anguilla Day**.

The **Leeward Island Cricket Tournament** is held on St. Kitts and Nevis each year in late May or early June.

JUNE

On June 16, Anguilla honors the **Queen's Birthday**.

The **St. Kitts Music Festival** is held each year during June.

A Calendar of Leeward Island Festivals

JULY

On July 7, Antigua and Barbuda observe **Caricom Day**.

On July 14, St. Martin, St. Barts, and Guadeloupe observe **Bastille Day**.

Schoelcher Day, a celebration in honor of Victor Schoelcher, the French parliamentarian who led the campaign against slavery in 1848, is celebrated July 21 on St. Martin and Guadeloupe.

The **Calypso Music Festival** on St. Martin is also held during the month.

AUGUST

The people of Anguilla celebrate **August Monday** on the first Monday in the month. On Nevis, horse racing is scheduled for the first Monday, to commemorate the emancipation of slaves in the British West Indies.

August 8 is **Constitution Day** on Anguilla.

SEPTEMBER

On September 19, St. Kitts and Nevis celebrate **Independence Day**.

OCTOBER

Antillean Day is observed October 21 on Sint Maarten.

NOVEMBER

On November 1, the people of St. Martin and St. Barts observe **All Saints' Day**, while Antigua celebrates its **Independence Day**.

The people of Sint Maarten and St. Martin keep November 11 as **Concordia Day**, a joint celebration of the long-standing peace between both countries on the island. November 11 is also **Armistice Day** on St. Barts.

DECEMBER

December 19 is **Separation Day** on Anguilla.

On St. Kitts, the annual **Carnival** is held from December 24 to January 3.

December 25 is **Christmas**, and December 26 is **Boxing Day**.

On St. Martin, St. Barts, and Guadeloupe, **Réveillon de Saint Sylvestre**, a New Year's Eve celebration with noisemakers and dancing, is held December 31.

Recipes

Fresh Salmon and Avocado Salad
(Serves 4)
12 oz fresh salmon
1 cup white wine
2 ripe avocados
4 hard-boiled eggs
Lettuce, tomatoes, and fresh parsley for garnish

Directions:
1. Poach salmon in water and wine to cover until it flakes easily.
2. Drain and let cool.
3. Flake into medium-size chunks and arrange on a bed of lettuce with sliced avocado, tomato wedges, and hard-boiled egg.
4. Season with one of two sauces listed below:

Sauces
Mix until smooth:
1/2 cup ketchup
1/2 cup mayonnaise
1 tsp lemon juice

or

Blend:
4 tbsp lemon juice
1/2 cup olive oil
1 minced garlic clove
1 tsp mustard
Salt and pepper to taste

Cockles and Mussels with Garlic
(Serves 4)
16 to 24 cockles or clams
12 to 16 mussels
4 cloves garlic
3 tbsp fresh lime juice
2 oz white wine
1/2 cup heavy cream
3 tbsp fresh basil
1/2 cup Parmesan cheese

Directions:
1. Clean clams and mussels.
2. Sauté garlic, add lime juice, wine, and cream. Bring to a light boil.
3. Add cockles (or clams), mussels, and basil. Cover and simmer for 10 minutes.
4. Remove cockles (or clams) and mussels and place them in an oven-safe pan.
5. Discard top mussel shell.
6. Add Parmesan to sauce and reduce by half. Pour over cockles (or clams) and mussels and sprinkle with additional Parmesan cheese and chopped basil.
7. Reheat under broiler.

Grilled Saffron Shrimp with Basil Tomato

(Serves 2)
10 large shrimp
1/2 cup butter
1 sprig saffron
3 tbsp lemon juice
2 tomatoes
1/2 cup fresh basil
1/2 cup fresh parsley
2 tbsp olive oil
1 tbsp bread crumbs
1 garlic clove, minced

Directions:
1. Peel and de-vein shrimp.
2. Melt butter, add saffron filaments and lemon juice, and heat. Marinate shrimp in this mixture for one hour.
3. Place shrimp on skewers and grill for three to four minutes, or until pink, brushing with butter marinade.
4. Sauté garlic in oil; add chopped basil, parsley, and bread crumbs.
5. Stuff mixture into tomato shells.

Rum and Banana Toasted Sandwich

(Serves 2)
1 ripe banana
Dash of cinnamon
2 oz dark rum flavoring
4 slices of bread
2 scoops of vanilla ice cream

Directions:
1. Mash banana in a bowl and add cinnamon and rum flavoring. Blend until smooth.
2. Butter one side of each bread slice. Spread mixture between slices of bread with buttered side out.
3. Place sandwich in toasting press, or toast in a pan, until both sides are light brown and crisp.
4. Place on a dessert plate and top with a scoop of ice cream.
5. Serve immediately with garnish of fresh fruit and powdered sugar.

Glossary

abolish—to do away with something completely.

archipelago—a group or chain of islands.

brackish—a mixture of freshwater and sea water.

buccaneers—pirates.

cannibalism—the practice of eating human flesh.

cays—low islands or reefs of sand or coral.

dilapidated—decayed, deteriorated, or fallen into partial ruin.

dominant—prevailing over all others in number, frequency, or distribution.

duty-free port—a port at which no taxes or customs duties must be paid on imported or exported goods.

effigy—an image or crude representation of a person, usually publicly burned in celebration.

gingerbread woodwork—decoration on the outside of a house or building that is showy and elaborate.

gross domestic product (GDP)—the total value of goods and services produced in a country in one year.

Knights of Malta—a Roman Catholic religious order that was founded during the Crusades, a series of wars fought by Europeans to recapture Jerusalem and other lands in the Middle East from the Muslims who held them. The Knights were dedicated to providing care for the sick; they also were well-trained soldiers who formed one of the strongest fighting forces in the world at the time.

petroglyphs—carvings or inscriptions on a rock.

Glossary

petroleum—an oily, flammable liquid that can be used to produce such products as gasoline, fuel oils, and lubricants.

prominent—notable, leading, or eminent.

referendum—the practice of submitting to a popular vote a measure proposed by a legislative body.

seclusion—the condition of being isolated from others; solitude.

topography—the visual representation of a particular place.

trade winds—prevailing winds that blow constantly in the same direction.

urban—part of a city, or related to city life.

vista—a scenic or panoramic view.

Project and Report Ideas

Reports

Write a report answering the following questions:

- How does life on the Leeward Islands differ from life on other islands in the Caribbean?
- What is different about the history, economy, geology, and culture of the Leeward Islands compared with the history, economy, geology, and culture of the other Caribbean islands? What is similar?
- Which island do you think you would prefer to visit? Why?
- Why do you think the Leeward Islands are not as well known as other Caribbean islands such as Jamaica, Bermuda, Aruba, or the Cayman Islands?
- If you had to write an advertisement for one of the Leeward Islands, what would you say to entice people to visit?

Write a description of the plant and animal life on the different Leeward Islands, answering the following questions:

- Which islands are lush and tropical, and which are more arid (dry)?
- Describe some of the different kinds of plants you would find on the different islands. Where else can you find these kinds of plants? Are any birds, animals, or plants "protected" on any of the Leeward Islands? Which ones?
- Sometimes, animals that are not native to an island, such as iguanas on Anguilla, find their way to different islands anyway. Why does this happen?
- What are the different type of fish and sea creatures you would find near the Leeward Islands? Are any of these rare? Are any of them found in other places in the world?

Boat racing is considered the national sport of Anguilla. In three paragraphs, describe how the races are conducted, what kind of boats are used, and the history of boat racing on the island. Also give information about where these boats are constructed, who builds them, and when the races are held.

Volcanoes and hurricanes are an inescapable part of life on the Leeward Islands. In a short report, describe some of the biggest hurricanes to come through this area of the Caribbean and which islands were most affected by them. Research the volcanic activity on Montserrat and describe what happened to the island in the late 1990s. Also answer the following questions:

- Why are hurricanes and volcanoes more common here than in other parts of the world?
- What other places in the world are also at risk for hurricanes and volcanoes?
- How are these areas similar to the Leeward Islands and how are they different?

The history of the Leeward Islands is tied closely to colonization and slavery. Pick one of the islands and write a short report answering the following questions:

- Which country settled the island?
- Did that country use slaves just in the Leeward colonies, or in other colonies as well?
- How did emancipation, or the freeing of the slaves, change the economy on this island?
- How is the history of slavery still observed today on the island?

Chronology

1775 B.C.	The Siboney Indians occupy Antigua.
35 A.D.	The Arawak Indians occupy Antigua.
1100	The Carib Indians overthrow the Arawak on Antigua.
1493	Columbus sights Guadeloupe, St. Martin, St. Barts, St. Kitts, Nevis, Antigua, and Barbuda.
1565	French explorer René Laudonnière discovers Anguilla.
1623	British arrive to colonize St. Kitts.
1631	The kingdom of the Netherlands occupies St. Martin.
1632	Great Britain claims Antigua.
1633	Spain recaptures St. Martin.
1635	French settlers arrive on Guadeloupe.
1642	The population of Nevis grows to 10,000.
1644	Peter Stuyvesant fights to capture St. Martin for Holland.
1648	Spain retreats from St. Martin; French and Dutch see the opportunity to claim the island, and the Dutch-French Treaty of Concordia is signed.
1648	The first French colony on St. Barts is established.
1650s	Colonization of Anguilla by British begins.
1651	St. Barts is sold to the Knights of Malta.
1656	Carib Indians raid St. Barts.
1673	Settlers from Normandy and Brittany arrive on St. Barts.
1690	Nevis is hit by massive earthquake; resulting tidal wave destroys capital city of Jamestown and sinks part of island.
1745	Anguilla is attacked by French but is held by the island militia.
1758	The British briefly take over St. Barts.

1782	The French capture fortress on St. Kitts and assume control of the island.
1784	France sells St. Barts to Sweden.
1785	The French again attack Anguilla but are stopped by an English frigate.
1793	British take over St. Kitts.
1833–34	Slavery is abolished in all British colonies.
1848	Slavery is abolished on St. Martin and Guadeloupe.
1863	Slavery is abolished on Sint Maarten.
1871	St. Kitts is placed in a federation with Anguilla and Nevis.
1878	France repurchases St. Barts from Sweden.
1943	The first airport is constructed on St. Martin.
1946	France joins St. Martin, St. Barts, and Guadeloupe together to form a département, giving them equal footing with the départements of continental France.
1967	In the Anguilla rebellion, St. Kitts and Nevis loses the third island. Antigua also attains self-government status.
1981	Antigua achieves full independence.
1983	St. Kitts and Nevis achieve independence.
1995	Volcano begins to erupt on Montserrat and eventually sends two-thirds of the island's population of 12,000 fleeing to neighboring islands.
1998	A vote in Nevis on a referendum to separate from St. Kitts falls short of the required two-thirds majority.
1999	Hurricane José leaves a trail of destruction throughout the Leeward Islands.
2003	In July, the Soufriere Hills Volcano erupts again on Montserrat.
2004	Alan Eden Huckle becomes governor of Anguilla in May.

Further Reading/Internet Resources

Doyle, Chris. *The 2002–2003 Cruising Guide to the Leeward Islands.* Dunedin, Fla.: Cruising Guide Publications, 2002.

Dyde, Brian. *Islands to the Windward: Five Gems of the Caribbean—Sint Maarten/Saint-Martin, Anguilla, Saint-Barthelemy, Saba, Sint Eustatius.* Edison, N.J.: Hunter Publishing, 1990.

Permenter, Paris, and John Bigley. *Adventure Guide to the Leeward Islands.* Edison, N.J.: Hunter Publishing, 2001.

Robinson, Bill. *A Winter in the Sun: The Pleasures (and a Few Pitfalls) of the Caribbean Cruising Lifestyle.* New York: Sheridan House, 1995.

Travel Information

http://www.geographia.com/antigua-barbuda
http://www.caribbeans.com
http://www.travelintelligence.net/wsd/places/plce_34.html
http://www.sabatourism.com
http://www.st-martin.org

History and Geography

http://www.innanen.com/montserrat/history/1870-1880.shtml
http://www.countryreports.org

Economic and Political Information

http://www.cia.gov/cia/publications/factbook/geos/nt.html
http://www.cia.gov/cia/publications/factbook/geos/gp.html
http://www.state.gov/r/pa/ei/bgn/2336.htm
http://www.state.gov/r/pa/ei/bgn/2341.htm

Culture and Festivals

http://www.st-maarten.com
http://www.gocaribbean.about.com
http://www.anguillaguide.com/main.html

For More Information

Anguilla Tourist Board
Marketing Office
111 Decatur St.
Doylestown, PA 18901
Tel: 267-880-3511
Fax: 267-880-3507
Email: anguillabwi@aol.com

Caribbean Tourism Organization
80 Broad St., 32nd Floor
New York NY 10004
Tel: 212-635-9530
Fax: 212-635-9511
E-mail: get2cto@dorsai.org

Embassy of Antigua and Barbuda
Chancery: 3216 New Mexico Ave., NW
Washington, DC 20016
Tel: 202-362-5211
Fax: 202-362-5225

Embassy of Saint Kitts and Nevis
Chancery: 3216 New Mexico Ave., NW
Washington, DC 20016
Tel: 202-686-2636
Fax: 202-686-5740

Montserrat Tourist Board
P.O. Box 7
Plymouth
Montserrat, West Indies
Tel: 664-491-2230
Fax: 664-491-7430
E-mail: mrattouristboard@candw.ag

Office du tourisme de Guadeloupe
43, Rue des Tilleuls
92100 Boulogne Billencourt
Tel: (33) (0) 146-04-00-88
E-mail: o.t.guadeloupe@wanadoo.fr

Saba Tourist Bureau
P.O. Box 6322
Boca Raton, FL 33427-6322
Tel: 1-800-722-2394
Fax: 561-488-4294
http://www.turq.com/saba/

St. Maarten Tourist Office
675 Third Ave., Suite 1806
New York, NY 10017
Tel: 1-800-786-2278
Fax: 212-953-2145

Statia Tourist Office
Oranjestad
St. Eustatius
Tel: 599-3-182433
Fax: 599-3-182433
E-mail: euxtour@goldenrock.net

Index

Index/Picture Credits

Contributors

Senior Consulting Editor **James D. Henderson** is professor of international studies at Coastal Carolina University. He is the author of *Conservative Thought in Twentieth Century Latin America: The Ideals of Laureano Gómez* (1988; Spanish edition *Las ideas de Laureano Gómez* published in 1985); *When Colombia Bled: A History of the Violence in Tolima* (1985; Spanish edition *Cuando Colombia se desangró, una historia de la Violencia en metrópoli y provincia*, 1984); and coauthor of *A Reference Guide to Latin American History* (2000) and *Ten Notable Women of Latin America* (1978).

Mr. Henderson earned a bachelor's degree in history from Centenary College of Louisiana, and a master's degree in history from the University of Arizona. He then spent three years in the Peace Corps, serving in Colombia, before earning his doctorate in Latin American history in 1972 at Texas Christian University.

Lisa Kozleski is a newspaper reporter at *The Morning Call* in Allentown, Pennsylvania, and has lived in and worked for newspapers in Colorado, Washington, Philadelphia, and England. She moved to the Philadelphia area in 1995, where she lives with her husband, John, and their dog, Kaia. This is her fifth book for young readers.